I0203248

THOUGHT PROVOKING

Aretha James

Thought Provoking
Published through Lulu Press

All rights reserved
Copyright © 2009 by Aretha James

Interior Book Design and Layout by
www.integrativeink.com

ISBN: 978-0-578-02210-9

No part of this publication may be reproduced, stored in a
retrieval system, or transmitted in any form or by any means
electronic, mechanical, photocopying, recording, or otherwise,
without the written permission of the author or publisher.

ACKNOWLEDGEMENTS

I am truly grateful for the different ones who have made a gigantic impact on this project. For the last five years several of us have adopted one another as family and come together during the holiday seasons. At our gatherings each participant has to showcase a talent, perform a talent or speak. My sincere gratitude and appreciation to my daughters, Kris Powers and Carmen Penny, for their unselfishness and unconditional love. A big thank you to my jewels, Monica Penny, Donte Penny and Tavarres Young, for their love and allowing Grandma to entertain them. They are uniquely different and exhibit awesome talents.

A special thanks to Ernestine Sayles and Don Wilson. We have come a long way since childhood. Thanks to Kayla Smith, Darlean Lee and Annie Wiley for continued support. Friends Erma Weekly and Mildred Jones who listened and critiqued from afar. Thanks to Carolyn Harrison who continuously encouraged me to write. Thanks to my very special friend, Hamin Shakoor, for pushing me and not allowing me to give up on a dream.

Special thanks to an invaluable writing group organized in 1995 in Atlanta, GA. Thanks to my church family, Faith Full Gospel Baptist Church, for giving me an opportunity to share my writings with a special thank you to a fellow writer, Alveta Bell. Thanks to a very dear sister, Dr. Shirley Jordan, who believed in me without knowing much about me.

This project would not have been possible without the support of the late Pennie Morris Allen, who was my greatest audience. Until 1998 every line written was read for her approval. Thank you Mom for being a great inspiration and a great listener.

Finally, thanks to Integrative Ink for the layout of this project and to Lulu Publishing for making it impressive and appealing enough which gave me the courage to publish.

My thanks to God for all things and making all things possible.

TABLE OF CONTENTS

THROUGH MINE EYES

Through mine eyes I am a nobody,
A somebody,
A junkie,
A whore,
A liar,
A thief.

Through mine eyes I am penniless
Smoking reefer,
Prescription drugs,
The uppers,
The downers,
The reds,
Heroin,
Crack,
Cocaine.

Through mine eyes I am ugly,
Too pretty,
Too short,
Too tall,
Too fat,
Too skinny.

Through mine eyes I see in others
The bad,
The ugly,
The depressed,
Low down
The useless.

Through mine eyes I live
On the edge,
Confrontational
Live for others
Selfish
Suffer low self esteem.

Through mine eyes what does it matter?
I am
What God says
I am
And it's
Through
HIS eyes
That matter.

LOOK AT ME

Look at me, a gnat
So insignificant until I attack.

Look at me, not at all pretentious
Or putting on an act.

Look at me, a butterfly.
That's blossomed into a beautiful
And colorful creature.

Look at me, a praying woman.
One with genuine features

Look at me,
Proud, bold and tenacious too.

Look at me, sticking to truth
Just like glue.

Look at me, what do you see?

LOVE IS

Love is more than holding hands.
Love is more than a walk in the park.

See inside of me.

Love is more than a soft tender kiss.
Love is more than a deep back rub.

Read my thoughts.

Love is more than a foot massage.
Love is more than a glimpse between rain drops.

Look at me.

Love is a sweet fragrance.
Love is a consuming flame.

See inside me.

Love is a memory as delicate as a bubble.
A bubble that can gently disappear.

Massage love and it will
With stand time.

I Dare You

I dare you to place my name in the
Atmosphere.

Whether a negative or positive

I dare you to look beyond me as if
I do not exist.

I dare you to engage in idle
Conversation in my presence.

I dare you to dream of our
Nation as one with diversity.

I dare you to dream.

PERSONAL

God has brought me to another hour in life.
An hour to heal.
He has brought me to an hour
To forgive.
He has brought me to an hour of prayer.
To an hour to share.
He has brought me into his personal fold.
My story has yet to be told.

ENDEARING LOVE

I have not loved so honestly as now.
Without reservation, I give all of me to you.

What do I see in you?
From your eyes, I feel warmth.
From your kiss, I feel compassion.
When you hold me, I feel safe.
From our conversations, I feel loved.

Oh how I love the feel of this endearing love.

BILLS

Bills, Bills, Bills
My life, bills.
My hobby, bills.
My lover, bills.

What's my name? Bills
Who am I? Bills
School, bills
Church, bills

My employment is to pay bills.

You don't try to make them.
They're just there.
In the most private places, bills.
Water bill,
Light bill,
Gas bill,
Sewage bill.

Wherever I am,
I must know there is a bill
There is no escape to
Bills, bills, and more bills.

As I Am

Love me
Don't try and change me.
Be kind.
Be loving.
Be giving.
Show compassion without expectations.

Hold me
Even though I may appear distant.
Distant yourself when I'm crowded.
Remember
It is not a
Problem with you.

THE HIDDEN AGENDA

Say it loud, I'm Black and I'm proud.
More power to the people was announced to the crowd.
Black is beautiful was the chant for all
The world to see that unity was the call.

With these messages came a multitude of changes
Because the constitutional amendments needed re-arranging.
Communities were infiltrated appearing respectable,
But there was a price to pay being proud and beautiful.

With unity came difference, diversities and oftentimes pain.
Unity, was it to be attained through selfish gain.
Was it Hitler, Stalin or Hoover that wrote the definition?
I say demand a re-write and establish your own conditions.

How Patriotic Must I Be?

My forefathers were brought to a foreign country against their will.
Towns, counties and cities they had to build.
They were forced to relinquish their names and religion.
Freedom was not home and they made no decisions.
Daily from sunrise to sunset this country was made to be
The land of the beautiful and supposedly the home of the free.

My people have been castrated, lynched, tarred and feathered.
We have been forced to step aside while others had the liberty
To do however they pleasured.
We have been forced to ride in the rear of the buses and share
Standing room with available seating yet paying the same fares.

Today the problem is not slavery, but the plight
In the Black communities throughout the major cities.
The handwriting is on the wall what is happening
And who is benefiting.

World war I Black soldiers fought in Germany
For a country that thought of us being less than human.
We've proven patriotism as participants fighting
Against Japan, Korea, Vietnam, and now Iraq.
Don't forget the Revolutionary, Civil War and Kuwait.

In predominantly Black universities, non Blacks' education is free.
How can I or my children get a free college degree?
If truth is told, we are and have proved to be one of the most
Patriotic group of people there are and no doubt ever will be
In this nation's history.
Many contributions have been made in this country
By the Black community.

Much is not recognized or advertised and is uncanny.
We have brought much joy to the homes of many
With music in all genres. The movement in our dance
And the move to the beat of the drum. We have advanced
In the sports arena and broke many a record.

Theater, radio, television and movies just to name a few
Areas where we are visible but recognition is long over due.
Sports, literature, medicine and recently the political
Arena which my parents would be tickled
And never could have imagined a Black man
Taking center stage as a presidential nominee as an American.

Am I angry? Am I disturbed? You got it right.
Question my integrity and patriotism and you've got a fight.
Why is it necessary for me to continue to prove who I am.
That behavior does not paint an intelligent picture for any man.

Tell me again, how patriotic must I be?

I Speak What I Know

Hide your head in the sand if you dare.
When you bring it out be aware
The story is the same
Regardless to which proper name
You give it to support freedom or guilt.
It still perpetuate the ugly filth
You are attempting to hide
From the ones who are on your side.

Whether acknowledged or not
Whether living in the cold or hot
The outcome will forever be truth
And in the spirit of truth is proof.
You are adamant in your conviction
That you speak what you know.
Let me help clarify some areas
Of your perdition.

You have a play on words either
To appear good or righteous.
Please take heed that neither
Can save you from a hellish
Reality. Get your story straight, so
Speak what you know.

BUTTERFLY

It was about noon when I spied that beautiful yellow creation.
Flirting about from one magnificent scene to another junction.

From its very unusual beginning who would think
The joy and beauty this creature would bring.

Not a care and not a notion of a worry
She makes her stops but always in a hurry.

Given a chance she will tarry along the way
So keep perfectly still and enjoy the parade.

In my yard today was an array of colors. Yellow, blue,
Multi brown, with orange. Just to name a few.

Darting from the flowers and through the trees
In playful competition with the bees.

Here comes the yellow one again. She's looking at me
Telling me to live and be free.

It's been said that the butterfly is good luck.
But what do I know? I dare not pluck

Or attempt to touch or catch one.
For there goes my luck oh son of a gun.

There is beauty in a small insignificant creature
That God made which blends with nature.

PROVOKING THOUGHTS

Why can't I love?
Is it because of my immaturity?
Maturity?
Am I set in my ways?
Can I not adjust?
Merely against change?
Against the same?

Why the discomfort with others?
Can I not think for myself?
Too technical you say?
Perhaps too slow?
Are my pains confusing?
Or is it my complaining that does it?

Am I only a babysitter?
What about signing for your loans?
Securing your apartment?
Don't forget the tax breaks?
Am I in your way?
Did I make your way?
Not agreeable, huh?

How did I get to where I am?
Was it a process?
Overnight?
Is my hair gray from worry?
Am I too old?
What is old anyway?
Am I too much of an expense?
Am I your tax write-off?

Did I get in your business?
Do you have any business?
Do you have the answers?
Oh now I talk too much?

Do you have a headache yet?
You better get you some business.

My Sanctuary

Inside of me is where I live.
Tucked away where there is little or no pain.

You may ponder as to why?

It's simply my safe haven.
It's my sanctuary and I have the control.

Nobody should have that control
Other than I.

WHO DECIDES

God's man is HIS love.
The decision to love man was not
Because of man's color or his size.

The decision to love man was not of his
Religious affiliation or whether
Man believed or not.

After all the design of man was made in the image of God.

The Jews are waiting for Christ the Messiah to come.
The Muslins believes that Christ walked on this
Earth as one of the Prophets.
The Christians believe that Christ was born, died
And was resurrected.

Who decides what is true?

Could it be that all is true?
Could it be for each group
What they think is what is real to them?
For some Blacks, many of the members in the
Bible including Jesus was Black.
What do we know?

Who decides what is real?

For eons children believed that a man with
A beard came from the North Pole
With his reindeers hitched to a sleigh.
He was to deliver gifts to all children
That had been good.

Many shed light on this outrageous story.
They decided to give this man some color.
The NOW generation told their children truth.

Who decides what's right and wrong?

Who decides what is right for you
And what fits your style and personality?
Are your decisions based on what you
Have heard, have read, have seen?
Perhaps it's what you feel.

Who decides?

We dark skinned sisters have been led to
Believe that we should not wear loud Colors.
Red should not be a color
In our wardrobe.

White after Labor Day is unheard off.
So if you have nothing else to wear
But what society dictates not to wear,
Do you not choose?

Who decides?

God is love.
Who do you love?
Do you love God?
Will you allow yourself to love?
Will your love be your car?
Your house? Your career?
Your wife? Your husband?
Your friend?
Do you worship and adore you?

Who decides?

I would honor and obey my parents.
Maybe my teachers
And seniors as well.
I could respect my boss.
My co-workers.
If I am nice, what would people say?
If I were prompt daily to work,
How would that appear to others?

Who decides?

I can earn at least six figures a year.
Does that mean that I must excel in my studies.
Does it mean I must go to class?
Does it mean I can cheat my way?
Are you not developing your mine and
Thinking for yourself?

Who decides?

Where there is gossip
Do you disassociate yourself?
Are you in the lead pulling someone down?
Are you basking in someone else's misfortune?

You got the picture.
Your destiny is in your hands.
You can make all of your dreams become reality.
Who decides where your hands will lead you?

I have heard that nothing is neither right nor wrong
But it's your thinking that makes it so.

JUST BECAUSE

Just because I do not have a lustful life.
Just because I do not laugh as I once did.
Just because I do not find the time to love.
Just because I am no longer on the dance floor.

Just because I have a head full of gray hair.
Just because my eyesight is dim.
Just because my memory fails me at times.
Just because my steps have gotten shorter.

Because I have multiple ailments from the lack of activity.

I should begin again to live.
I should begin again to laugh.
I should begin again to dance.
I should find time to love.

The gray hair is less important.
The eyesight improves.
The memory lapses becomes fewer.
Your pace increases.

Just because is no reason to continue on a downward trend.

My Soul Is Resting Now

At last I am at peace because my soul is resting.
There is nothing that can be said to disturb this peace.
Many times I thought I had left you, but for
Sure my soul is resting now.

Shhhh, can't you hear me speaking?
Was I a mother, a sister, an aunt, a cousin, a
Grandmother, a friend or an enemy?
Which was I to you? Did I leave a negative image
Or a positive image with you?
My soul is resting now.

If I hurt you, if I offended you in any way, if I didn't
Smile when you thought I should, if I showed no
Remorse at your sadness, if I failed to hug you or tell
You how much you were loved, oh I am so sorry.
You see my soul is resting now.

We have shared in laughter as well as tears.
We have had fun but we've also shared sad times.
Can you hear me speaking?
It's my soul that's resting and not your.
I am at peace. You see my soul is resting now.

PLEASE ANALYZE

Sister are you bitter? Are you angry? Do you have an attitude?
Sister do you have reasons for your actions?
Sister should you be bitter? Should you be angry?
Sister should you have an attitude?
Sister please analyze.

Sister rid yourself of the headaches and heartaches.
Sister rid yourself of all of the extra baggage causing pain.
Sister choose to live a long and eventful stress free life.
Tap into what makes you happy. Tap into what makes you smile.
Sister please analyze.

Watch eagerly how we as sisters respond to one another.
We respond with less than enthusiasm. We respond uncaringly.
Sister we breathe and bleed the same. We have the same problems.
Why look beyond another as if they are non-existent.
Sister please analyze.

Sister enter into the recesses of your mind and internalize where you are.
Is there a pattern? Why the differences? Why are you alone?
Is alone what you really want or need?
How do you perceive yourself?
Sister please analyze because you have the control.

SELF-ESTEEM NO STEAM

Self esteem is to know who I am, who I was, and who I will be. Self esteem is to know where I am, where I've been and where I am going. Self esteem is to know the expectations of myself and expecting nothing from anyone else. Self esteem is to know that I am responsible for my own happiness. Self esteem is to know in order to get, I must first give. Self esteem is to know to have a friend, I must show myself friendly. Self esteem is to know what I want, when I want it, where I want it, why I want it and how to get it. Self esteem is not compromising my integrity for the sake of anyone else. Self esteem is about loving thy neighbor as thyself.

SO, WHO AM I?

I am a beautiful Black woman with a strut that emulates the arrogance of a banter rooster. I glide as if floating on a cloud over a serene deep blue ocean as I watch the sun fall behind the horizon. Oh, how peaceful. I am like a stallion strong and tall with a long slender crane neck with skin of ebony shining like charcoal.

SO, WHO AM I?

I am as precise as the point of a needle with a mind just as sharp. I speak with eloquence what I know, when and if a situation warrants an opinion. I can dine with elegance in the presence of the most affluent and feel right at home and very comfortable eating ribs and chicken and liking my fingers. I expect nothing from anyone because it is nothing to me anyone would owe. I give out of love not expecting to be reciprocated. I have been hungry enough to accept hand outs from my in-laws. I stand to be corrected and give respect to ones who agree to disagree.

SO, WHO AM I?

Often, as allowed, I will shut down and go into myself and think. There are also times when I don't have nor do I want any steam. It seems that I have all of the answers, have it all together. But no, at times I have a problem. I lack APPLICATION.

SO, WHO AM I?

LORD, I'M FOR REAL THIS TIME

I have been before you numerous times and here I am again. I give it all to you and then I take it back over and over and over again. Through each mess you've kept me. I fall on my knees for forgiveness and before a week goes by I'm right back in my mess again.

You see these tracks on my arms or what was it that I digested or inhaled? Was it the rock or the pain medication brought off the street? It was an attempt to flee from me.

Lord, this time I am for real.

I have given over to you all of my upsets, all of my heartbreaks, and all of my disappointments. At the time, I really meant it but I took the upsets, heartbreaks and disappointments all back. Lord you are my hope, you realize my dreams and are everlasting. Although life at times have seemed hard and hopeless, I've always known that there was hope.

Taking from the candy store started my one profession. I graduated soon afterwards to larger and more expensive items. You've been my protector all of this time but I know time is running out.

Lord, this time I am for real.

While alone, you've been the friend when it was difficult to maintain a human relationship. When there was nobody to confide with, I got comfort knowing you were near. I have wasted too many sleepless hours, empty days and meaningless relationships. It hurt so badly at times but I knew it was all in your hands because you had the power to conquer my fears, my loneliness and my emptiness.

I've been told often that I don't need anyone but you. Well that's not true at all. I need others in my life. How can I share and with whom will I share with being alone? How can I trust or be a friend if there isn't anyone else?

Lord, this time I am for real.

Broken promises I have given to you. Like Peter, I have also denied knowing you. I promised to trust you and I did until Satan showed his ugly self. I know Satan is here to destroy me and to destroy my family. Although he is my adversary, I yet allow his control of me.

Lord I know you protected me in my escapades with multiple partners. But you saved me from a disease that's running rampant in our society. Was I promiscuous because of a lack of attention or perhaps a little too much of attention? Only you know why I chose my path.

Lord, this time I am for real.

I had to sink real low this time. I didn't think I could pull myself back together. I know it's you keeping me, loving me and holding me in your arms. I remember falling on my face and crying out to you. You know that I need humans too, but where are they? We have no trust for one another. Keep me safe and removed from jealousy and envy. Do whatever you have to do.

I have done much damage with my tongue. I have lied. I have lied. I have lied. What a misunderstood and misdiagnosed weapon. Lord, give me another chance to do what you require of me. I'll get it right this time.

It's me again Lord, but I am for real this time.

My Soul Cries Out

Back during the times of Grandma and Grandpa I would
Hear someone wail 'My soul cries out'. Not sure of
What it meant, but each would say 'just keep on living'.
Today, oh Lord today, Lord I fell on my face today
When I heard the cries of my people.

My heart hurts for our young parents. Unless rooted
In the words of God, on bended knee daily with
Your families, Satan will snatch, grab and nibble
Until nothing is left.

How long must I toil down here? How long must my brain
Be over-taxed and picked? How long must these
Clouds hang low? How will I know? Hear me this day.
I now know what Grandma and Grandpa meant for like
Them my soul now cries out to you.

ARE WE SPEAKING

We must leave an inheritance for our children's children. What will they inherit from us?

Are we speaking of possessions? Of course we are. The ability to gain ownership and prominence. The ability to earn our money, share and invest our money.

Are we speaking of attitude? Of course we are. The ability to have control of our way of thinking and to believe all things are possible.

Are we speaking of ingenuity and creativity? Of course we are. The ability to know who we are and who we can become and to have the resources and know how to accomplish our desires.

Are we speaking of independence and autonomy? Of course we are. The ability to be a leader without thinking of the obstacles that lies ahead and to have the freedom and liberty to be successful.

Are we speaking of acceptance? Of course we are. The ability to receive one on his or her own merit.

Are we speaking of imagination? Of course we are. The ability to see the future as we think it should be and to have the freedom to use our mind set.

Are we speaking of indifference? Of course we are. The ability to show concern and interest for others regardless to who they are.

Of course we are speaking of faith. The ability to take God at His word. The ability to step out on nothing and believe that something is there.

JUST LOOK AT ME

You sat next to me without acknowledgement. Did I do something to you? I ask myself this question but the answer is that she didn't see me.

Oh no she's not having a conversation with the lady in back of me. Perhaps I have an odor or bad breath. But I brushed my teeth and freshened up prior to leaving work today.

She's yet to make eye contact with me. What could be the problem? It's time for scripture. I failed to bring my bible, but she has one. For sure she would not mine my looking on with her.

As she flips through pages I inch a little closer to see the Word, but yet keeping my distance. She moves inconspicuously to where her back is facing me ever so slightly.

I know what that means. Why won't she just look at me. I'm sure she has noticed what I am wearing. My jeans are a little tight and I am showing a bit much cleavage. These stilettos are killing me. Of course this red hair isn't helping my image at all.

She's not judging me or is she? Why won't she just look at me. Perhaps she doesn't want to look at me for fear that I may see the real her.

I need a smile today, a howdy or a hello. My world could prove to be a bit better with that. I spent the night in a shelter. The clothes are those of a kind lady at the shelter therefore all that I had.

I am hurting. If she would just look at me she would see this. I had one disagreement last night too many. I had an altercation with my live in boyfriend and was thrown out on the street to fend for myself. If she would just look at me. I need a smile, a howdy or just a hello. Please look at me.

SKY

Oh God a story is told through your clouds

I understand why and how sky blue can represent peace. Try looking up when there are no clouds on a bright and sunny day. You can get lost in God's wonder.

It's an awesome sight. It's an awesome feeling. It is like I am being absorbed in God's love. He has encamped His love all around me.

Now come with me. When there are white clouds with a sky blue background, What do you feel? What do you see?

I feel comfort. I want to rest. Imaging being in the midst of the clouds and God with His love is rocking me in the cradle of His arms.

A little gray is added to the clouds which may result in rain followed later with more sunshine. In life troubles and hard times come and go but you can always look forward to brighter days.

207 AND HOLDING

The top count on electoral votes has been 207 for at least fifteen minutes now. What's the problem? Just in the last five minutes the bottom number has jumped from sixty something to a hundred.

Tick tock, tick tock. Twenty minutes, twenty five minutes the top number yet holds at 207. Tick tock, tick tock. My heart is pounding. I can't stand the anticipation any longer. 207 and still holding. That bottom number has moved one thirty three, one thirty five, but the top is yet at 207.

Tick tock, tick tock. Only 63 electoral votes needed to declare a winner. I'm sick, I'm tired and disheartened. What's the problem? The top number is yet holding at 207.

Tick tock, tick tock. Aha the count from the West coast is coming through but very slowly. America we have ourselves a new president. 207 is no longer being held.

The Reality Is

So your boss is from the same persuasion as you. Why not give the same respect as one with a different persuasion.

If I am the same as you, why is it necessary to react to me differently? You question everything I say or do.

Am I asking for special privileges? Not at all. I'm just another employee working toward the same end as you.

The reality is that we have a common goal which is to collectively get a job done. The ultimate is to handle basic needs.

Why is it so difficult to face our realities?

KINDRED SPIRITS

On the cemetery grounds of my forefathers, I stood fighting back tears of jubilation but yet sadness. What an honor to stand at the gathering of the off-springs in the midst of the cemetery. There was a certain kinship with each name read. Unlike the Kookaburra where its cry sounds like someone laughing loudly, the dead were crying out but with a sadden bellow.

I could hear from afar a passionate cry for families to be mended. Fathers go home and take your wife and children with you. Prevent your children from running aimlessly in the wilds without direction. Trust in the Lord with all your heart and lean not to your own understanding. There is another cry in the distant that compels the children to honor their father and mother and to obey. Yet another cry in the far distance saying I don't feel no ways tired and I've come too far to turn around now. In unison with a loud thunderous sound I hear beautiful melodious voices singing LOVE IS THE ANSWER.

There is no piano. There are no drums. There is no orchestra. There is foot stomping and hand clapping. It's been said and I concur that a dose of laughter is good for the soul.

Close your eyes and go with me using your imagination. Can you feel them? The earth that we tread is the very dirt that our loved ones once treaded upon. Feel the dirt. Remove your shoes and let the dirt run between your toes. Feel the humiliation they must have felt at times not having control of their own lives. Look into their eyes. Is there pain, joy sadness, happiness, peace or love? Can your imagination take you back to slavery? What do you see? Are there whelps, tears, or blood? Were they caught trying to flee the Massa?

Saints they were not but many of us today would wish to think otherwise. If we knew our past, it's possible we would not be so judgmental today. If our past was known, perhaps cycles that exist now could be eliminated. If we knew our past, teen pregnancies, drug abuse, depression, murder, suicide, alcoholism, adultery and many other isms could possibly be eradicated. IF ONLY WE KNEW OUR PAST, we could perhaps have a present.

For me the experience in the cemetery was a kindred of spirits. A plethora of emotions flooded my soul and placed me on a voyage of change, commitment and clarity. At my low moments, a walk on those grounds will allow me to come to myself and visualize my life looking from the outside in.

Art Of Meditation

Someone asked a question of me once, how can you always appear so calm and relaxed? Needless to say at that time, I didn't realize how I was being perceived. After that initial question, I began to analyze and realized a gift had been granted and loaned to me. I realized during times of turmoil and uncertainties in my life that I had found myself fervently praying whether at work, driving, in bathrooms, exercising or anywhere. I would engage in positive conversations and steer clear of the negatives. I would try to find the good in every aspect of being and would concentrate on a Bible passage that had a meaningful definition to me.

Yes I do become riled, but through the years those occurrences have lessened. I find that I'm in control most times and can dictate who can occupy my space. I believe each person has the ability to control their life through meditation. The method used for meditation may vary depends on what works best for each person. Some would say that I use a relaxing technique others would say I use prayer but then there are others who would label me as being a little insane.

There are times when I can empty my mind, thinking on absolutely nothingness. I can set myself outside of a situation to see a broader picture, which allows me the opportunity of being an on-looker on what is going on in my world. It appears as if I am standing on the outside of a very tall wrought iron fence encasing a moat and castle having the ability, with today's technology, to observe the goings on in each room. Each of these rooms has its own symbolic definition.

In the last couple of days I have observed harmony, joy, hope, power, beauty, endurance, faith, humor, love, respect, humility, determination, and peace just to name a few in my castle. Oftentimes I will either pick myself a bouquet of wild flowers or simply purchase a ready-made bouquet at the local grocery store as a reminder of the simple things of life that cost very little. I am focusing on the yellows, the reds, the pinks and array of colors in my bouquet. It is life, very lively and bright. In addition to my bouquet which helps to stage the other events in my castle, is the ability to see clearly obstacles coming my way. The viewings in my castle has helped me to realize that even though God has predestined my life, I am guided by the compass that I read.

Viewing each room in my castle as if through today's technology helps me to realize that my service is to others. My service is not haphazardly done but deemed mandatory for the progress of this world. Through meditation I know that **"I cannot direct the wind, but given an opportunity I can adjust the sail"**.

DIFFERENCES

A problem exist between the man and woman and the boy and girl. Is this a true or fair statement? If the relationship between the sexes is questionable, it is reasonable to believe that this issue began at a very early age. These persons did not become adults and suddenly could not communicate. An adult cannot be shaped and molded into something that is totally foreign without apprehension and frustration. Personality changes must occur while those young mines are yet impressionable and still have the time to improve without feeling threatened.

There are many reasons for the differences, however, reasons are not warranted solutions are. No one person is to blame, but everyone is at fault. That saying about "it takes an entire village", well this is where we all come up short.

In the 1990's society, man and woman are seriously fighting for that competitive edge to see who ends up as number one. This competition has moved from the board room to the bedroom. The woman is busy getting attention and making her presentation to earn her piece of the pie. On the other hand, Mister doesn't want the noise, he is contented just the way things are, nor does he want to share his pie.

Neither chooses to see that it only takes both compromising and working toward that common goal to accomplish their desires. Each must get a grip and come to terms with the part their mate is to play in his or her life. Each must be allowed to make decisions and feel that they have value. The business and personal relationship should be based upon mutual respect. The business part of the relationship should not spill over into the personal which is an unconditional relation opposed to spilling into the business relation which is conditional.

Each party must reach a consensus and be in agreement on what is/is not business and handle each situation accordingly. In a personal relationship it is not necessary to have written divisions of responsibilities but there must be mental divisions. If there is a lack of knowledge, it is up to the partner to share information that will make the other party equally knowledgeable.

Without the giving of one hundred percent in a relationship between both sexes, the relationship is doomed to failure. Neither man nor woman should be allowed to feel used or mentally abused because one or the other is not exercising sound judgment in decisions being made in the relationship. Each one should have a feeling and sense of belonging and harmony.

LOVE WITH AN ATTITUDE

In your tender lean years while growing up, did you not enjoy dining out at Mickey D's, Burger King, Taco Bell or other more elegant eateries? Were your clothes not clean and without holes even though they did not carry the designer label? Occasionally were there not items with designer labels, handed down by your grandmother's employer, that you wore proudly?

Did you not relax in your own room with your very own television and stereo? My-oh-my were you deprived? Did you not have a telephone with your very own number? Was your linen not clean and changed weekly? Were you not provided with heat in winter and a bright light to brighten an otherwise dimly lit room during dark hours? Were you reasonably comfortable in summer from the simmering heat?

What Do I Owe?

Were you not given a curfew and grounded if the curfew was broken? Were you not encouraged to study and be your best at whatever choice you made? Were you not expected respectfully to do school work and housework each day before your leisure? Did you not spend your summers, if warranted, in summer school? Vacation bible school? Traveled via train, bus, airline or automobile to visit family and friends?

Were you not compelled to correspond with your dad? Were you not punished for not sending him that special occasion card or writing that letter? Were you not told to give your dad and opportunity to fulfill your many needs by soliciting his help by mail?

What Do I Owe?

How much time was spent in my room on my bed talking into the wee hour of the night? Can you remember how many subjects were discussed at the kitchen table? Do you remember the special meals shared at breakfast, lunch or dinner? Do you remember family and friends sharing meals with us at Thanksgiving and Christmas? What about other occasions? Did you not get your share of Father John, vitamins or cod liver oil to ward off viruses?

Were you not filled with embarrassment by the many visits made to your school, but in the same breath elated that time was taken? Were you not aware of the calls made to and from your teachers regarding your behavior? Were you not given a chance at the time to explain and redeem yourself?

What Do I Owe?

Were you not proud to be fitted for your first bra and embarrassed by the first tampon fitting that was ushered into place? Who helped to twirl the rope for double dutch? Who sat on concrete to play jacks and pick-up-stick? Who played hop scotch, jump rope and dodge ball with you? Have you gotten more upset with anyone else while playing one of your favorite games like monopoly or aggravation? What about chasing the tennis balls hit beyond the fence? Can you count the many scars from roller skating on the side walk or laughing at me as I attempted to relive my youthful days? Who did you scare out of their wit while teaching you to drive?

Would you say that you were knowledgeable about your heritage? Were you not shown the livelihood of the rich as well as the poor? When visiting the less fortunate areas of town where ones lived under card board in the park or in areas where there was no grass, did you not realize how close you were to poverty? Upon your return home, did you not realize how rich we were not of where we lived, but because our freezer was filled and our space was not cramped?

What Do I Owe?

Who encouraged you to read if only the comics? Who always said "you are smarter than that"? In your plot to run away from home, who advised you that you owned nothing, but would be allowed to keep what you were wearing? Were you not reminded that just because mother's thought their children beautiful, was not an indication that everyone else felt the same?

Were you taught that you should elude adversity, but defend yourself if needed? Was your privacy not respected? Was thank you and please reciprocal house hold words? Were you taught that in order to love another, you must love yourself? Were you not encouraged to honor any commitment voluntarily made? Were you taught to share your knowledge by passing it on? Who taught you that respect for oneself would mandate respect from others? Who said it was not necessary nor important to be liked by that you should demand respect?

What Do I Owe?

Who was present for your first date? Who went shopping with you for your prom dress? Who was available to pick you up when you fell or kissed your scratch to make you feel better? Was I not there with the hug you needed when you had that spat with the boyfriend or suffered a broken heart? Were you not shown love? Were you not told that you were loved? Were there conditions placed on loved like 'if' and 'but'? Were you not allowed to express yourself regardless to the circumstance?

What Do I Owe? How Can I Pay?

Children are quite impressionable and parents have certain responsibilities in the growth and well being in their maturity. However upon their reaching adulthood, parents are no longer responsible for them. Our children must realize and be willing to accept that decisions made affects their entire life.

Love and respect is what I owe. Love and respect is what I have to give. In order for our children to maintain independence, I suggest the debt is settled. The bible states "to whom much is given, much is required". It's best not to be in debt with anyone.

If we as parents continue to give, our children become indebted to us.

How Can You Pay? You Would Owe. Be Independent. I Dare You.

Boy To Man To Marriage

This article was written and passed to my daughters with the hopes that they will raise my grandsons in a manner that any young woman will take pride in having either of them as a soul mate.

It is important that a male child is in touch with his feminine side but it must be kept in perspective. If the feminine side is kept dormant as a child, as an adult your child may not realize a need to show compassion. He may not understand seemingly insignificant nothings. He may be inconsiderate to the needs of others. He may be insensitive to ones that are not as strong whether mentally, physically or spiritually. Let me share my definition and thoughts on what being in touch with the feminine side means.

A boy should have responsibilities that will allow him to function autonomously as an adult. He should know everything about the kitchen which would include cooking and cleaning afterwards. He should know how to do laundry. He should not be allowed in his bed without a bath or shower. He should be make to pick up and clean up after himself, which includes giving the bathroom a good scrub. He needs to know little and insignificant things to help prepare him for the multiple obstacles he must face.

A young man should be taught as a boy that he possess an abundance of physical strength. Strength that is admired when polished and refined as a form of fine art. Therefore taught that physical strength should not be used to bully or intimidate but to be admired as the piece of art that it is.

As a child, his thoughts should be permitted to be expressed and acknowledged as important. To broaden his world and increase his vocabulary, he should be exposed to the arts, theatre, nature, family and many cultural events. Growing up he should be taught to take nothing for granted for through his travel he would see how others live. He would see folk living in over-crowded project, families living under card board boxes in the parks, some living very modest and others in more affluent communities.

A boy should be allowed to show his emotions without feeling belittled. He must know that he has a right to cry and as an adult male crying does not dictate he being any less of a man. Some would measure a need to cry equally with a need to laugh or an orgasm. Deep and hearty laughter is good for the soul. A good laugh is an experience of sheer ecstasy with rest which brings renewed energy. Whether tears of joy or sadness, a heavy load is lifted from the heart after a good cry. If that child holds back the tears, those emotions can manifest themselves and be performed in an aggressive manner.

Be truthful and be fair with your son. Parents, when you have wronged your child, please apologize. Remember, we are all human and expected to error. When your son does well, please praise him. When he falls short of your expectations, enlighten and encourage him. When he goes against the grain and you realize his reasoning, introduce him to different options. If his reasoning is not sound but hopelessly bleak, get yourself additional reinforcement.

Each young man must know the differences in a rose. There is the rose that is showcased but is being choked by thorns. Unless relieved of the thorns, the beautiful rose will be trampled and caught up in the confusion of the thorns. On the other hand, there is a rose with all the spacing but droopy and sad. This rose only need to be cultivated, watered and nurtured to become a prize winner. This is the rose that the young man will showcase. He must know that each woman is special and should be respected and showcased.

Each of your sons needs the influence of a positive male role model through out childhood leading into his adult life. Fathers should take an active role in the life of his son. It is not enough to just pay the bills. Your son needs the discipline that only his father can give. He needs to know that he is loved by his father without any conditions whether he reaches dad's expectations or not. After all they are dad's expectations. Teach your son the importance of keeping his word and that his character is built based on his honesty and integrity. Your son learns from his dad's habit, good, bad or indifferent. Your son learns trust, distrust, love, hate, truth, or lies. A young man will emulate what he has seen, therefore it is very important to surround your son with positive attributes and positive people.

If possible mothers, in the single parent homes, should solicit the assistance from extended male family members. A grand father, an uncle or a close male family member can fill the void if the father is not involved. Mothers should not speak negatively to your son about his dad. Share some of the good times and good things you had with his father. If you know it's not logical or economically feasible to buy Fila or Air Jordan's, be honest with your son. If dad is not paying child support and you have solicited the courts for this to be done, let your son know this. Let him establish some opinions of his own. Whatever the question, answer as honestly as possible.

Finally, what is being done with our young men is no longer working, perhaps it is time for another change. We know getting to real manhood is impossible with out having a direct line and being in constant communication with God. Our sons must know that God is real, God must be feared and God is the only answer.

FINAL SAY

I see the questions on your faces.
Why like this? What's with the Jazz?
Everything is upbeat and happy.
She was God loving and God fearing.
Could this really be what she would want?

Give not my loved ones a hard time.
Respect them because they are respecting me.
I was positive and not negative.
I was filled with life and not a recluse.
I enjoyed adventure and spontaneity.

Allow this celebration to be filled with
Laughter, happiness, joy, and peace.
Let this celebration be positive.
Let participants be reminded of life
And adventure. After all
The sorrow is when you are yet here.

What a joyous crossover.

My Prayer

My Father who sits in the heavens and who with omnipotent power made the heavens and the earth. My God who took a void and made a creation. My God who placed the stars and the moon in particular form to guide through darkness that was created as night. My God who placed the sun in the sky to provide heat and light and to distinguish the void from night. My God who placed the oceans and seas in just the right locations to help maintain growth.

Father please bless our world leaders that decisions made are to edify your kingdom. Let your kingdom come and let your will be done. Bless our country, our heads of state and municipalities to enrich your people so that your people can enrich the church. Let your kingdom come and let your will be done. Bless your people to do the upkeep of your kingdom.

Give me a clean heart oh Lord and renew a right spirit within me. Wash me, purge me and make me clean. Although born into sin, give me a repentant heart. I pray that I make a 180 degree turn not to deviate from your path of righteousness. Shape me, make me, mold me as if I am clay, bake me, and paint me. Make me as a new creation in you because old things have passed away.

You are wonderful and ever present. You are an awesome God. You are bad and bad all by yourself. There is no one like you. You are a healer, my lover, my friend, my peacemaker, my doctor, my lawyer and my all in all. I am so proud and blessed to be a part of you.

You are my father who accepts me. You are my daddy who loves me as his little girl but respects me as a woman. You kiss my tears and mend my broken heart. Thank you Lord for giving me assurance that you love me. I don't have to guess or wonder.

God let the contents of this book be an inspiration to many.
Amen

www.ingramcontent.com/pod-product-compliance
Lightning Source LLC
Chambersburg PA
CBHW032036090426
42741CB00006B/836